THE ILLUSTRATED HISTORY OF

BUSES AND TRUCKS

NICK BALDWIN

Foulis

Haynes

A **FOULIS** Motoring book

First published 1987
© Nick Baldwin 1987

Published by:
Haynes Publishing Group
Sparkford, Nr. Yeovil, Somerset
BA22 7JJ, England

Haynes Publications Inc.
861 Lawrence Drive, Newbury Park,
California 91320 USA

**British Library Cataloguing in
Publication Data**

Baldwin, Nick
    The illustrated history of Dennis trucks.
    — (A Foulis motoring book).
    1. Dennis trucks — History
    I. Title
    '629.2'24   TL230.5.D4
    ISBN 0-85429-622-0

Library of Congress catalog card
number 87-81364

Editor: Robert Iles
Page layout: Tim Rose
Printed in England by: J.H. Haynes & Co.
Ltd.

Introduction

Dennis started out on its long and fascinating career from a popular spring board – the bicycle. Unlike all its early contemporaries in Coventry, the Dennis brothers set up shop in a county town within easy striking distance of London. Guildford may not have had much heavy industry but it was at the centre of a rich hinterland.

From motor bicycles and tricycles before the turn of the century, Dennis Bros turned its attention to cars and then, in 1904, to commercial vehicles. It never went through the dead-end steam phase and, even more remarkably, it never used the primitive chain drive of its rivals. The Dennis patent worm-drive axle brought silence, efficiency and reliability to trucks and buses for the first time: this feature helped to make Dennis one of the largest heavy vehicle makers in the First World War and the years that followed.

Dennis' early interest in fire engines soon developed and it established a reputation as an important supplier in this field that has been retained to the present day. Although Dennis cars were discontinued in the Great War, the firm quickly became one of the largest British producers of military trucks.

Afterwards, it managed to avoid the recession that hit all its rivals by building high quality, but competitively priced, trucks and buses. The factory was fortunate to be in an area that recovered more quickly than the industrial north of England – the traditional home of heavy vehicles – and by the late 1920s the firm was undoubtedly Britain's most successful producer of trucks. Dennis came close to acquiring Guy and even to merging with Leyland in this period.

The fire appliances and municipal vehicles that had been a natural sideline to the truck business from the early 1920s stood Dennis in good stead through the lean years of the 1930s. Unfortunately, its trucks and buses were in a less happy position. Dennis was slow to develop a successful diesel engine and lost out in the heavy bus and truck field to firms like Leyland and AEC. In the lighter 2 to 3 ton field, where it had always been very successful, it was suddenly faced with competition from vast American-backed rivals like Ford, Dodge and the new Bedford.

The Second World War, when Dennis built thousands of trucks, trailer fire pumps and specialist vehicles, disguised the true state of affairs at Guildford but by the 1950s the company was no longer a force to be reckoned with in the general transport field. A foothold was kept in the heavy bus market with Bristol designs made under licence, but normal haulage vehicles dwindled and only sales of municipal types remained buoyant.

Having neglected the top-weight truck market, which was by then the only safe preserve of the specialist manufacturers, Dennis made a last ditch attempt in the late 1960s to interest operators in the Maxim range, powered by Cummins and Perkins V8 engines. Both engines were new and largely untried in service, and Dennis did not prosper on the outcome.

The Dennis brothers had died in 1939 and it looked to be only a matter of time before their famous firm followed them. However, in 1972 a last minute reprieve came with the takeover by Hestair. With new management and drastic economies Dennis survived and started the spectacular recovery that brought it back into the truck, bus and coach fields with a range of vehicles that neatly fitted niches left by the giant international motor firms, both in Britain and in many export territories.

In the following 180 photographs, many of them never before published, I have attempted to show the enormous diversity of Dennis vehicles made in the past 80 years and to give an idea of the firm's successes and failures in the extended captions that accompany them.

Dennis is a unique independent vehicle maker with a long and remarkable career. I hope you enjoy seeing and reading about the Dennis range as much as I have enjoyed delving into the firm's past.

John Dennis, born 1871 in Bideford, North Devon, worked for a Guildford ironmonger in 1894 and made bicycles in his spare time. In 1985 he started the Universal Athletic Stores in the town and made motorised machines from 1899. This is one of his first four-wheelers of 1900, made with help from his younger brother Raymond. Most early machines had De Dion engines and about 200 were sold in 1902.

In 1904 Dennis patented the worm gear rear axle they had introduced during the previous year. It gave a quieter and more efficient drive than the chains used by most of their rivals in both the car and commercial vehicle fields, and gave enough reduction for a direct top gear to be employed.

DENNIS

Inset above:

The first commercial vehicle was a 15 cwt van for Harrods in 1904 and other famous customers followed. This was W.H. Smith's first petrol driven motor van, a four-cylinder 12 hp machine. Most of the early vehicles were powered by Simms, Tylor and Aster engines.

Inset above right:

In 1906/7 Dennis sold buses to the Netherlands, Italy and Brazil, following successful British sales from 1904. The first vehicle consisted of a horse-bus body on a motor chassis for Ben Richardson's Kingston to Richmond service. Here we see a 28 hp machine built from scratch as a bus later that year, when it cost £715 plus lettering.

Main photograph:

1908 saw the first of a famous line: this fire appliance equipped with turbine pump was purchased by the city of Bradford. Raymond Dennis was in Kiev at the time negotiating an order for seventeen 35 hp cars (the same engine was also used in 3 ton lorries).

Above: Many big fleets of Dennis vehicles were ordered in the early years. In 1909 McNamaras had about 100, many of which lasted to 1925, and MacFisheries kept 20 1910 Dennis going until 1936. By 1912 Harrods had 16 Dennis vehicles, Maples 18 (including a 40 hp car for the boss), Carter Paterson 23, London County Council 14, Bristol Tramways 14 and the Metropolitan Asylums Board 42, of which several are shown here (the odd ones out are a Leyland and a Serpollet steamer).

Below: Cars continued to be manufactured until the 1914-18 war, Grand Duke Michael of Russia having bought no less than three. White & Poppe engines were used from 1906 and this type of engine was standardised for all vehicles in 1909, when Dennis employed 400 men at Guildford and made this magnificent example.

Opposite page: All sorts of special vehicles were made in the years before the 1914-18 war. There was a rear-engined tractor, a combined tractor and irrigation machine and these export vehicles able to run on paraffin. The upper one is a forerunner of the dumptrucks that were developed in America in the 1920s.

THE "DENNIS" TIP WAGON

Especially built for The Crown Agents for the Colonies

Capable of carrying 5 tons   Can turn in 30 feet
Driven from a Paraffin Carburetter
Price of 40 h.p. 4 5-ton Chassis complete with Body   **£800**

In the test this Vehicle accomplished 41·75 gross ton miles per gallon, with an average
speed (loaded) of 10·85 m.p.h. and maximum of 12 m.p.h. over hilly country

Built especially to the order of The Nile Gold Mining Co., Ltd.
Price, fitted with very wide Metal Wheels (rear wheels shod with wood
blocks) and with Paraffin Carburetter   **£590**
Built to carry 2 tons over Sand

11

Taxis were quite a popular Dennis sideline as this group of 18 hp machines in Dundee, Scotland, confirms. They cost £430 complete, or £10 less without a roof over the driver! The specification was broadly similar to the Colonial 18 hp car. 24 mpg was said to be possible 'under favouring conditions'.

1910, when this photograph was taken, saw the completion of this new assembly area, followed in 1911 and 1912 by the construction of 47,000 and 30,000 square foot buildings on the present site. The 2,000th vehicle was made in 1912 at a time when Dennis was finding it difficult to sell as many chassis as White & Poppe's output of large engines. Dennis were on a par with Leyland in terms of output, and were more successful than their near neighbours, Thornycroft, at the time.

DENNIS

Opposite page top: This splendid advertising van was built on the 14 hp 8/10 cwt chassis of about 1908. The chassis cost £305 plus £36 for Dunlop tyres and £40 for a standard body made in Dennis' coachworks.

Opposite page bottom: A 1912 charabanc for a local operator (or jobmaster) on a 3 ton chassis; a similar chassis was accepted by the War Office for its military Subsidy scheme in the following year. In 1913 Dennis Bros. became a public limited company with capital of £300,000. The first year's report revealed profits of £43,250, followed by £61,500 in 1914 and £117,220 in 1915.

One of the last peacetime vehicles of 1914 was this double decker, seating 18 passengers outside and 14 inside. It had a 35 hp White & Poppe engine and was bought by West Bridgford. The worm drive continued to appeal on account of its quietness in towns and Pierce-Arrow in America recruited H. Kerr Thomas from Dennis in 1910 to help design this and other features of their truck range. He returned to England and joined AEC in 1920.

The first turbine pumpers were supplied to London Fire Brigade in 1910 and other satisfied users at the time included Glasgow, Leeds, Birmingham, Penang (Malaya), Rowley Regis, Christchurch and, not surprisingly, Dennis' own brigade. Here we see a staged callout from the works entrance at Woodbridge, Guildford.

Another famous early Dennis user was Pickfords. This is a typical three-tonner with the usual features of a ball bearing four-speed gearbox with direct top, White & Poppe single-jet carburettor and T-head engine, Bosch magneto, leather-lined cone clutch and, of course, worm gear axle protected by patent 3224. The rod shown under the chassis was anchored to a 'horn bracket' to locate the axle against torque and braking reaction.

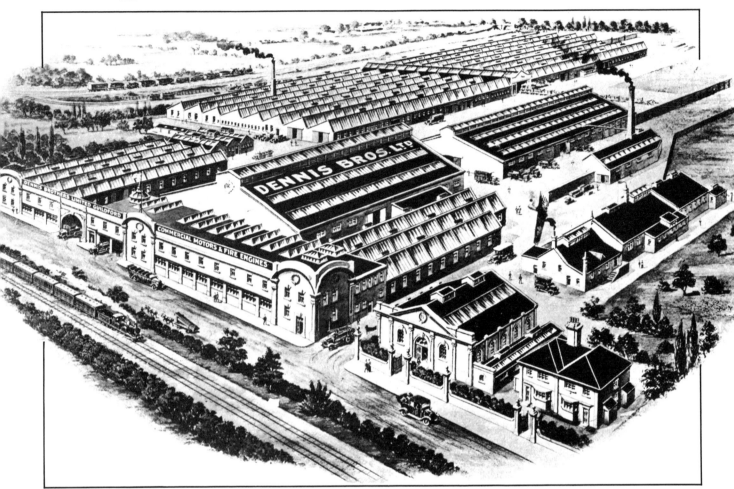

Left:
In 1900 some twenty men were employed in a factory extension built in the garden of the Athletic Stores making bicycles, Universal motorcycles, tricycles and quadricycles. Capital grew to £30,000 in 1901 for expansion and premises were taken at Bridge Street and Onslow Street. Then in 1905 the Torrey Alexander Mission Hall in Brixton was purchased and transferred piece by piece in Dennis trucks and rebuilt at Woodbridge Hill on the outskirts of Guildford. Around it had grown this sizeable factory by 1915, most of which was little changed externally until the mid 1980s.

Opposite page bottom: A glimpse under the bonnet of the famous Model A War Office Subsidy chassis. The army regarded it as a three-tonner but for civilian use Dennis usually quoted $3^1/2$ to 4 tons. This is Captain Davis inspecting one during a 1914 subsidy trial at Putney.

Above and below: What Captain Davis saw under the bonnet (which has conveniently been removed for the purposes of these photographs). It is a four-cylinder T-head, 40 hp White & Poppe engine of 6.235 litres capacity, with exhaust on the nearside along with the magneto (mounted, one would have thought, rather vulnerably near rain that could be blown through the radiator). Above the exhaust valves are compression/priming taps to aid starting. The oil pressure gauge is read through a hole in the scuttle.

Above: Friend or foe? A Model A poses with some heavy fire power. Some 7,000 lorries were supplied by Dennis in the Great War, putting them level or a little ahead of the other large British producers like Albion, Thornycroft and Leyland but behind the new mass-producer AEC. The latter managed to produce 3,000 more, thanks to a moving production line.

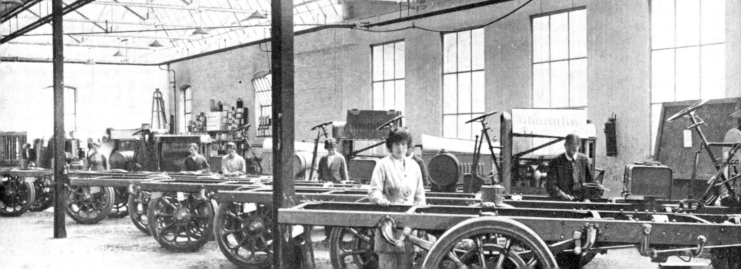

Above and previous pages: Woodbridge Hill Works had expanded in the Great War to employ 14,000 men and women. Here we see the machine shop, case hardening department with gas furnaces and oil tempering baths, and the paint shop (the photographs date from 1920, but this was still more than ten years before spray painting was considered). Profits averaged about £100,000 per annum during, and soon after, the Great War and were maintained in the slump of 1921/2. In this period, orders fell to 25 chassis per week (though output was kept at about 50) and the workforce at Guildford was reduced to 700.

Main picture:
Swords into ploughshares – or one of the things to do with an ex-War Department chassis in the early 1920s. Motor charabancs became popular with operators and customers alike and if demand was slack in the week a lorry body could often be substituted. This looks like the annual outing of the Paxton Arms regulars – one hopes they have left room for the crates of Cannon ale!

Inset:
In 1920 Raymond Dennis left for a 60,000 miles round-the-world tour to drum up exports and was knighted the same year. He was the sales expert and more outgoing than his brother, who was the gruff engineer. Here is a special six-tonner of that year for Buenos Aires, complete with a radiator badge in Spanish. Six-tonners had Y-spoke steel rear wheels, but were otherwise similar to three- or four-tonners.

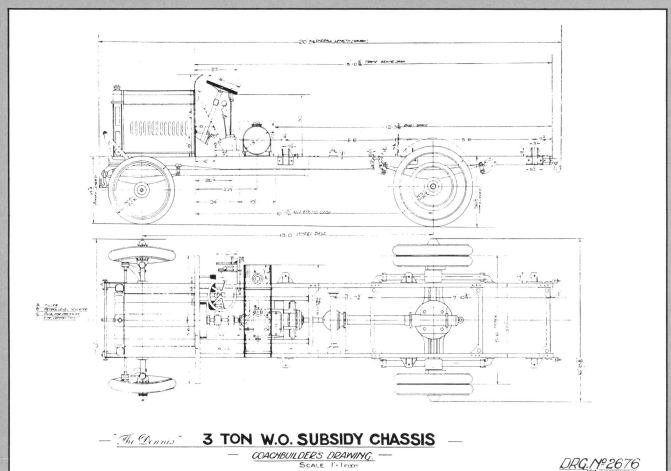

— *The Dennis* — **3 TON W.O. SUBSIDY CHASSIS** —
— COACHBUILDERS DRAWING. —
SCALE 1"=1 FOOT

DRG. No 2676

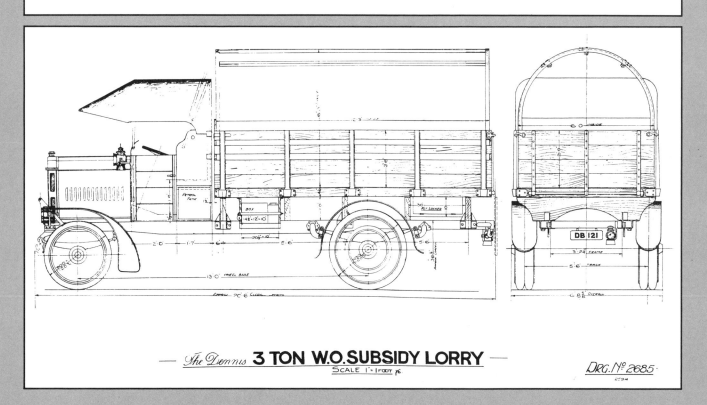

— *The Dennis* **3 TON W.O. SUBSIDY LORRY** —
SCALE 1"=1 FOOT

DRG. No 2685

Opposite page: These are the plans of the Subsidy Model A as supplied to coachbuilders, showing it as bare chassis and also with standard War Office bodywork. If it complied with WO requirements the operator received £110 spread over three years in exchange for six-monthly inspections. If it was 'called up' for military use 7$\frac{1}{2}$ per cent was deducted for each six months of its age and then 25 per cent added to arrive at the purchase price, so long as this did not exceed its original value.

Below: Technically very similar to the subsidy chassis was the 40 hp 30-seat charabanc chassis. Here we have a 1921 example with Dennis-built body. It had a governed top speed at 1,000 rpm of 16 mph. To make it more stylish than rival types on ex-WD chassis it had a smoother radiator shape and a rounded and tapered bonnet. The wings were also more streamlined.

DENNIS

Right: The chassis of a 30-seat charabanc in 1920, showing that it had the advanced feature of a self-starter (note flywheel ring gear). Like the subsidy lorry it had dispensed with the horn bracket to locate its rear axle, which was now attached to a half-length torque tube.

Bottom: As well as three-tonners Dennis made a few two-tonners in the Great War. 27 of the larger type were provided with W.A. Stevens petrol-electric drive, several of which were used as buses by Cardiff Corporation. Dennis also made pumping sets for drinking water on the Somme front. Fire engines continued to account for between 50 and 100 sales per year throughout the 1920s and here we see one for Trinidad at the 1920 Commercial Motor Show, Olympia. Behind it are a 3 to 4 ton van and 5 to 6 ton lorry.

Right: Capital in Dennis Bros Ltd increased to £600,000 in 1919, '1913' being dropped from the title in this year. The money was used to buy White & Poppe Ltd and P.A. Poppe then became a Dennis director, though his firm remained in Coventry for twelve more years. Light trucks were having a difficult time against cheap ex-WD types and imports and in 1920 Dennis formed a separate marketing company to compete in the cut-and-thrust world of car dealers who had begun to sell trucks. Great Portland Street was synonymous with the car trade, hence the location and title. Only 2/2½ ton and 20/25-passenger models were sold at £1,000 per chassis through a chain of Dennis-Portland dealers. The idea was not a success.

Opposite page:
New fields were urgently needed for Dennis' large output of chassis. In 1921 their first vacuum cesspool emptier was made at the request of High Wycombe RDC. In 1922 motor lawn mowers with White & Poppe engines, trailer fire pumps with Dorman & Blackburne engines, and this street-washing machine arrived. It could sprinkle to a width of 50 feet or use more concentrated jets for washing or fire fighting (225 gallons per minute at 85 lbs pressure). In 1925 similar machines with the addition of gulley emptying equipment were offered. Note the worm drive trademark used on all literature.

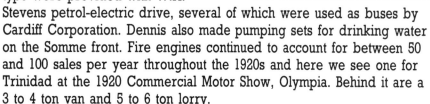

The DENNIS

PATENT
CONVERTIBLE STREET WATERING
AND WASHING MACHINE AND
THREE-WAY TIPPING WAGON

Made in Two Sizes—with a Tank Capacity of 900-Gall. and 1200-Gall., convertible into a 3½-4 ton and a 5-6 ton Three-way Hydraulic Tipping, or standard hinge-sided Lorry Body respectively.

Telegrams: "DENNIS," GUILDFORD
Telephone: 575 (4 lines) GUILDFORD
Cables: A.B.C. 5th Edition, LIEBER'S, BENTLEYS and MARCONI

DENNIS BROS. LTD.
Guildford, England

27

ALL COMMUNICATIONS TO BE ADDRESSED TO THE COMPANY AND NOT TO INDIVIDUALS.

PIONEERS OF THE
WORM DRIVE.

THE OLDEST MOTOR MAKERS
IN ENGLAND.

ESTABLISHED 1895

Dennis Bros. Ltd.

COMMERCIAL MOTOR & FIRE ENGINE MANUFACTURERS
PIONEERS OF THE TURBINE FIRE PUMP.

GUILDFORD.

CONTRACTORS TO
BRITISH ADMIRALTY.
H M GOVERNMENT
INDIA OFFICE
WAR OFFICE
COLONIAL & FOREIGN
GOVERNMENTS
ETC ETC ETC

Telegrams :-
DENNIS GUILDFORD
Telephone :-
575 (4 lines) **GUILDFORD**.
A.B.C. Code 5th Edition.
LIEBER'S 5 LETTERS.
BENTLEYS. MARCONI.

IMPORTANT **WHEN REPLYING PLEASE QUOTE REFERENCE**

RDg DB

12th June 1922.

Austin Farrell, Esq.,
Secretary to the Harbour Board,
Waterford, Ireland.

Dear Sir,

Your name has been kindly given us by Mr. Flemming the
Borough Surveyor and we hear that you are interested in a small
Turbine Pump suitable for washing down purposes and we enclose
leaflets dealing with our small range of appliances.

You will note you can purchase a light 2-wheeled trailer
type capable of pumping 250 gallons of water per minute. This
can be quite easily pushed about by two men or trailed behind a
car, the price being £450.

An alternative would be the light portable set which can
be carried by two men, which pumps 100 gallons a minute.

On the other hand, we can fit a Turbine Pump to a Ford
Car. This perhaps would really be the best in your case.

Hoping therefore that you will glance through these leaflets
and if you will favour us with your definite enquiry we shall be
glad to give the matter very thorough attention.

Yours faithfully,
DENNIS BROTHERS, LIMITED.

R Downing

Director.

Client's Vehicles are driven by our Staff at Client's own Risk and Responsibility.

Opposite page top left:
New postwar models included a chassis for London double deck bus bodywork from 1922 and a six-tonner of 1923 with 127 x 180 mm bore-and-stroke 60 hp engine (normally used in fire applicances) designed for trailer towing. Here we see a double decker with Strachan & Brown body in use with Biss Bros in 1924. This style of four-tonner based vehicle passed Scotland Yard's stringent requirements with minor modifications and was known by Dennis as their London Type.

Opposite page bottom
Another new 1923 model was a 20/25 cwt light lorry/van chassis. It had a 2.724 litre 34 bhp engine, in-unit gearbox and sold for a very competitive £295. Though about £50 cheaper than rival Vulcans and Guys it could not hope to tackle the Ford TT nor indeed the Morris Tonner, new in 1924. Only 28 sold but they prepared the way for a very successful 30 cwt model late in 1925. Here we have one of the latter machines, unusual in having solid tyres when most were on pneumatics.

Right and opposite page top right:
An interesting diversion in 1922 was the willingness of Dennis to fit its pumps to smaller, cheaper vehicles than its own chassis. Despite the Dennis name and trademark on this leaflet the vehicle shown is a Model T Ford. A letter accompanying the leaflet to the Harbour Board at Waterford recommended either this model or a cheaper 250 gpm trailer pump at £450, or else a 100 gpm portable set. One wonders what Waterford actually purchased.

The " Dennis " Turbine Pump, which can be fitted to any make of Motor Car

Telegrams : "DENNIS," GUILDFORD
Telephone : 575 (4 lines) GUILDFORD
Cables : A.B.C. 5th Edition, LIEBER'S, BENTLEYS and MARCONI

DENNIS BROS. LTD.
Guildford, England

The Admiral fleet in London was the first to get police approval for pneumatic (Dunlop) tyres in 1925. It was feared that buses might lose control or capsize if tyres punctured, but in fact their extra grip actually improved safety. The Admiral fleet's owner, A.T. Bennett, stands beside one of the twelve 30/55 hp buses he acquired at the time. In six months they had covered 371,280 trouble-free miles. It took three more years before double deckers could have similar tyres.

The London Type double decker based on 4 ton lorry components gained pneumatic tyres in 1928, when many earlier examples were converted. The arrival of roofs on double deckers led to an increase in track from 5ft 6 ins to 6 ft 2 ins for added stability. A similar machine was found and restored by the late Prince Marshall as the only survivor of a once popular type.

In late 1925 the old 40 hp engine was redesigned as the monobloc C with revs increased to 1700 rpm, at which 70 bhp was developed. One of the first recipients of this engine was the first drop-frame Dennis, their very successful E Type. It had four-wheel servo brakes made under licence from Rolls-Royce. The body on this example is by Brush of Loughborough.

A 1927 E Type in the livery of an important Dennis customer. This one has 35-seat bodywork by Dennis. The familiar worm was underslung on the rear axle and the top of the frame for most of its length was only 2 ft $1/2$ in above ground. Admiral, whom we have already mentioned in connection with pneumatic tyres, was the first to gain approval for four-wheel brakes (on an E Type) in London in 1926.

Inset left:

The C engine was further modified as the D in 1928 and, like the C, it came in various capacities to cover as much of the range as possible. The E Type chassis was offered with normal control as the F from 1927 and both types were used for goods as well as passenger work. The servo brakes were activated by clutches engaging in the gearbox that rotated the brake mechanism in proportion to the weight on the brake pedal. There was still full (though tiring) mechanical control, even with the clutches worn out.

Inset right:

We have all heard of tilt cabs, but this is ridiculous! Presumably the driver's seat was in the front compartment of the dustcart body. As the Dennis range expanded so did its fortunes. In 1927 its profits were £335,000 and it nearly acquired Guy. In the following year profits had risen to £361,000 and serious thought was given to a merger with Leyland in 1929. Even in the depths of the Depression £136,000 was earned in 1931. Unfortunately, excessive dividends were paid (100 per cent in 1933) which stinted later technical development.

Opposite page: An attractively bedecked 30 cwt model publicising Castrol's part in the King's Cup Air Race. To save money the spare tyre carried by this model was normally of solid rubber, but presumably Castrol were not as penny-pinching as some 'hire and reward' operations. This example has the 36 bhp 85 x 120 mm version of the C engine.

Above: A 30 cwt model in a different guise as a 16-seat bus. It was supplied to an Anglesey operator in 1926. From 1927 a new generation of the Dennis family, Royston Dennis, joined the firm and was on the

board from 1929 to 1960. In 1927 the ninth factory extension since the outset was built, adding 90,000 square feet. 1928 saw King George V grant his Royal Warrant for the supply of lawn mowers and a 30 cwt baggage van.

A low-frame version of the 30 cwt type came in 1927 and was known as the G, followed by the GL in 1929. The non-stop drive advertised in this Southdown GL sun saloon sounds rather alarming, even if 2/6d (12$\frac{1}{2}$p) was not a lot to pay! Ringmer Races for 4/- (20p) was perhaps a better day out.

Total output at Guildford in 1928 was in excess of 100 chassis per week.

A sumptuous Parlour Coach incorporating the Dennis F-Type Chassis. Owned by the Westminster Coaching Services Ltd., it is one of a fleet of this make operating between London, Cambridge, Newmarket and Bury St. Edmunds.

"F" STANDS FOR "FORTUNATE"—

But it is the "Fortunate" who sit in an F-type Dennis coach! The springs of many chassis are merely designed to spring, but those of the Dennis are designed to absorb road-shocks, and result in gloriously smooth riding. Minor vibrations from the engine are prevented from reaching the chassis by the spring-mountings which support the unit. ★ ★ ★ ★ ★ ★

Four-wheel brakes, low load-line and low centre of gravity are other points about the F-type that convert a chance passenger into a "Dennis Fan."

BATH & WEST
SHOW.
STAND
204

For full particulars of this or any other model, write to Dept. "M.T."

BRIEF SPECIFICATION:—

Wheelbase, 16 ft. 7½ in.; pressure-gun lubrication; frame height, 25 in.; 4-cylinder ("D"-type) engine developing up to 70 b.h.p.; detachable cylinder head in two parts; 4-speed gearbox; Dennis high-efficiency underslung worm drive; foot brake, servo-operated to all four wheels; pneumatic tyres 38 × 7 in., straight-sided single front and twin rear, with spare.

CHASSIS PRICE - £885

BROS., LTD., GUILDFORD

Motor Lorry Manufacturers to H.M. the King.

Opposite page: The normal-control version of the E introduced in 1927 was called the F, and latterly the FS, before it was discontinued in 1930. Only about 150 were sold but, as can be seen in this May 1929 advertisement, it was an attractive vehicle.

Below: In 1927 a special version of the E Type chassis known as the H Type was developed for double deck bodywork. The same 5.7 litre engine was used, as was the remotely mounted constant mesh gearbox with its short propshaft and fabric couplings linking it to the cone clutch. The servo brakes were the same but there was a wider front axle (6 ft 5$\frac{3}{4}$ ins) for stability. This is one of a batch of 17 supplied to Walsall in 1928/9. It has remarkably streamlined Short Bros 52-seat bodywork.

WHITBREAD

DENNIS

DENNIS

Depôt
Crown Bre
King Edwards
Birming

PF 5586

P.977

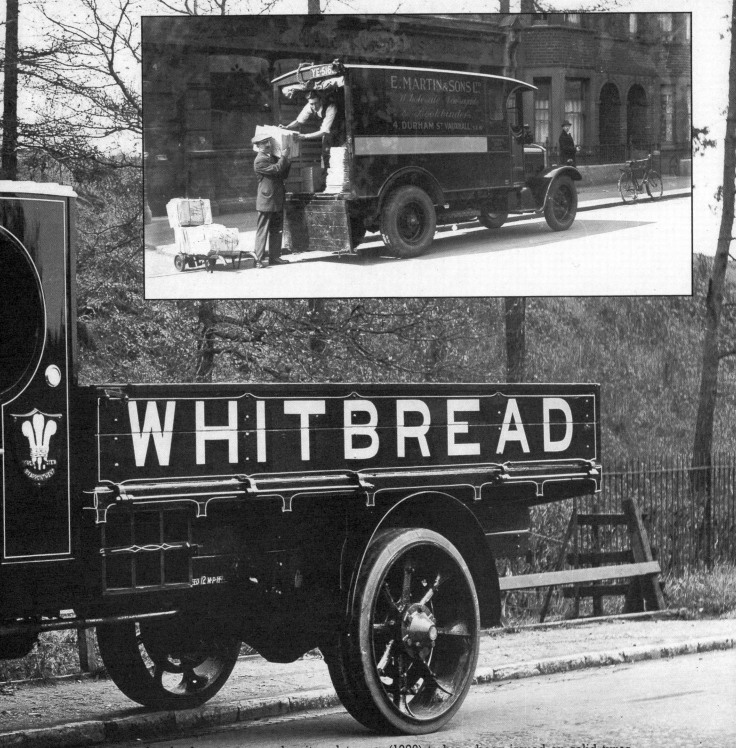

A splendid example of a four-tonner, and quite a late one (1926) to have been issued on solid tyres. Whitbread were keen Dennis users and had more than 60 at the time. The four-tonner, with the latest technical and styling updates, survived right through to 1934, about 800 having sold in the last ten years of production.

Inset: Here we have a pneumatic tyred 30 cwt van showing its typical solid spare tyre. Its registration number places it in about 1927 when such features as open cab sides, oil parking lights and bulb horns were still commonplace. Note that it also has electric accumulator sidelights which probably soon dimmed after the engine was turned off and would not have charged adequately in London driving conditions. Several London firms supplied vans on contract hire from the 1920s and in 1929 Dennis started its own hire-purchase subsidiary, Dennis Contracts Ltd.

DENNIS

BUILT BY
PHILIP WILSON
LIMITED.
ROCHESTER Rd. N.W.

MOTOR "BP" SPIRIT

PETROLEUM SPIRIT HIGHLY INFLAMMABLE

4818

BRITISH PETROLEUM
COMPANY LTD

U.W.   F.A.W.
        R.A.W.
        R & W.

Inset left:
The Co-op Societies were enthusiastic Dennis buyers and found them to be reliable, economical and priced below most of their rivals. By 1926 there were over 1,000 Dennis vehicles in Co-op service, of which about 500 had been bought in the two previous years alone (in preference to the Societies' own Bell brand of truck). This is a pre-1928 example with internal petrol filler rather than the external scuttle cap that was introduced in that year. If the vehicle is stuck the crew do not look too worried about the fact!

Inset far left:
Apart from the largest six-cylinder machines, most fire appliances shared components with the normal goods and passenger range. This one is probably a 250/300 gpm machine based on a shortened G chassis. It had aluminium bonnet and bodywork and a radiator cast specially in brass. Since 1925 Dennis had made its own pumps based on the Italian Tamini design. Dennis' fire appliance expert left to join the Birmingham Brigade – where this machine was in service – and, following disagreements with his old employers, promptly switched to Leyland vehicles.

Main photograph:
In 1928 a three-axle version of the regular four-tonner appeared. It was for 6/7 ton loads and had the usual 110 x 150 mm bore-and-stroke D engine. Only six appear to have been sold, including a cesspit emptier and this handsome Wilson-built tanker. Note the fire screen behind and beneath the cab isolating it from the risk of fire. The exhaust outlet was also in front of the screen.

Inset right:
The H double decker (which continued to September 1929) was joined in late 1928 by a development known as the HS. The first one was fitted with the C engine but the rest were provided with the improved D unit until the end of the model in 1930. Unlike the H it had Dewandre vacuum servo braking with wider drums. The radiator was more rounded with its securing bolts hidden behind an aluminium fairing. The familiar Dennis name in flowery script appeared for the first time on this model. This example has a Brush body.

Inset far right:
Although covered tops were becoming universal, and were even acceptable for red tape infested London operation, the LGOC for some mysterious reason selected this archaic design in 1929. The chassis is however the latest HS and not an H. A final updated batch on the H theme was made from 1930 to 1932 but only 40 of these HVs were built, compared with over 100 HS types.

Main photograph:
An interesting contrast with the earlier solid tyred Whitbread four-tonner is this 1930 six-tonner. In just four years, the cab has been enclosed, oil lamps have gone and pneumatic tyres have become almost universal. The six-tonner used the same 110 x 150 mm 50/70 hp engine of its smaller sisters.

P.2146.

P.3130.

DENNIS

Showing the low loading-height of the Dennis 7 cubic yard Refuse Collector. It is 52 ins.

THE NEW

DENNIS

LOW-LOAD-LINE
REFUSE-COLLECTING-MACHINE

is the product of a firm having 34 years' experience in the Motor Manufacturing Industry ; this indicates the thoroughly sound engineering practice that characterises the chassis and ensures long and trouble-free service.

The all-metal body of the machine is specially designed, from an intimate knowledge of Cleansing Authorities' requirements. It is low, light and capacious, and may, if required, be fitted with metal covers for dustless loading.

CAPACITY,
7 CUBIC YARDS.

WEIGHT,
WITH CANVAS COVERS,
UNDER 2 TONS.

TAX, £25 P.A.

4-CYLINDER ENGINE DEVELOPING 36 B.H.P.

SILENT WORM DRIVE.

HYDRAULIC END-TIPPING GEAR.

TAPERED BODY.

UNOBSTRUCTED REAR FOR EMPTYING.

LOADING HEIGHT, 4 ft. 4 ins.

The same chassis fitted with a sheet-van body for Commercial work.

For full particulars of any Municipal Vehicle, viz., street-watering and washing machines, gulley and cesspool emptiers, tip lorries, buses, tower wagons, ambulances etc., write to Dept. "M.T.,"

DENNIS BROS., LTD., GUILDFORD

Motor Lorry Manufacturers to H.M. The King.

Opposite page: Municipal vehicles comprised a steady and reliable market for Dennis, who came up with various ideas to ease the loaders' task. This 1929 advertisement shows a mini-wheeled model that was really just a variation on the 30 cwt chassis theme. It is interesting to see it in local haulage guise as well. Note the recently acquired name style and Royal Appointment coat of arms.

Above: The E was modernised in 1929 with the same Dewandre servo braking system of its double decker sisters and with this chromed radiator shell. The driver sat nine inches further forward than before and the wheelbase had increased by six inches, allowing fifteen inches more body space. 32/34 seats could be accommodated, though there was also a normal-control version with the old radiator shape called the FS that could seat up to 30. This example was photographed in July 1929, when Aldershot and District ran 230 Dennis buses.

A new overhead-valve engine in 1929 improved the performance of the two-tonner and its GL passenger counterpart. The gearbox was in-unit with the 85 x 120 mm bore-and-stroke engine, which developed 42 bhp and could average 15/16 mpg when the vehicle was laden. The chassis price was only £420 and this included servo brakes, though admittedly only on the rear wheels.

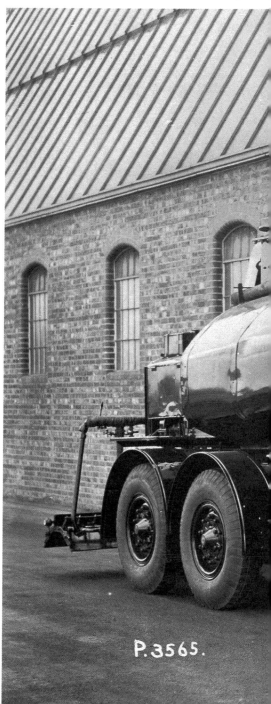

P.3565.

Opposite page top: A curious demonstration took place in the car park at Woodbridge Hill Works, Guildford before this cesspool emptier was despatched to Rotherham. The trolley and ramps were carried on the vehicle and enabled suction pipes to be handled with ease and to reach distant manholes. Capacity was 350 gallons, or 550 in the case of the gulley emptier version. Larger emptiers with street-washing capabilities went up to 1,200 gallons capacity.

Opposite page middle: Forward control versions of the four- and six-tonner vehicles, as well as drop-frame versions based on the bus chassis, were offered. This appears to be a four-tonner built from the outset for haulage with a straight chassis. Whitbread also used several similar chassis in both 4 and 6 ton sizes.

Opposite page bottom: The EV chrome frontal treatment and set-forward driving position were also applied to the double deckers. This HV for London service with Golden-Arrow looks rather odd with its open cab arrangement, though the LGOC purchased some with enclosed half-cabs in 1930.

Below: In 1927 Kirkstall designed a double-drive bogie with three differentials for use with an intended Dennis M Type 75-seat bus. This project never materialised and instead just two vehicles emerged with 108 bhp six-cylinder engines as tar sprayers for the Gas Light and Coke Co. in 1930.

The 8 litre side-valve engines were used up in various other models, notably fire engines, for several years from 1929, but only about 100 were built.

Below: 1929 was the year of six cylinder engines at Dennis. One of the engines was a 6126 cc overhead camshaft unit developing 100 bhp that was used in the Arrow 32-seater, launched in November. This had an offset driveline for the first time on a Dennis, which permitted a lower gangway. Park Royal built the body on this 1930 example for Salford. The Arrow was 6 cwt lighter than the EV but more expensive. In fact at £1,100 for the chassis it was directly comparable with the AEC Reliance and only 58 were sold up to the end of the model in 1935.

Right: Another six-cylinder design of 1929 was the 85 x 120 mm bore-and-stroke (4.1 litres) unit developing 65 bhp fitted to the Dart. This was a 20-seater based on the chassis of the four-cylinder GL which, like the Dart, had a push-rod ohv engine, though with only four cylinders and an output of 42 bhp. This was a smooth and lively performer but only 99 sold through the Depression to the end of the model's production in 1934. This example has lost its Dennis and Royal Appointment badge.

Opposite page bottom: The Dart, which incidentally was the first Dennis with a model name, soon received the radiator styling treatment of the larger Dennis passenger models. This 1931 example remained in service to 1940. The model was good for a little over 50 mph, which suited some coach operators and drivers with sporting inclinations, though perhaps not the passengers.

DENNIS

When is a Dart not a Dart? When it is simply an ohv four-cylinder GL masquerading behind the Dennis passenger range's family look. This 18-seat example started life in the Imperial fleet and is shown in its new London Transport livery in 1933, by this time looking a little battered. When the London Passenger Transport Board was formed in 1933 Dennis accounted for more vehicles (222) than any other make in its fleet, apart from AECs.

A bonnetted version of the Arrow was introduced in 1930, mainly for export customers. Like the forward-control version, it was

based on a modified EV chassis but had the new ohv 100 bhp six cylinder engine with in-unit gearbox and single-plate clutch. 56 mph was claimed for the aptly named Arrow.

Solid tyres were still useful on small-wheeled forward-control low-loaders when this one was sold in 1932. Dennis had built several for municipal work and many other stop/start delivery and collection services

found them useful. This example is a two-tonner. Two hundred were sold in the model's run, between 1930 and 1934.

An unexpected use for the 100 bhp Arrow in 1932 was as an ambulance. Whether it was intended for large scale disasters or collecting several out-patients for hospital treatment is not recorded. In any event its performance must have been impressive. At the Dennis works a further 60,000 square feet of factory space was brought into commission that year, plus a new case hardening shop.

The double decker version of the Arrow was the Lance, which was introduced in 1930. It shared the Arrow's ohc engine, as did various contemporary lorries and fire engines. This 1931 advertisement demonstrates a special feature of the engine whereby the camshaft could be hinged to one side to allow the head to be lifted. Durban specified some of these double deckers with Armstrong-Saurer diesels and in 1933 Dennis became the only British firm entitled to use these units in passenger chassis (apart from the Saurer licensee Armstrong, Whitworth, who mostly concentrated on trucks). Later, when its own diesel was proved, Dennis cancelled its agreement and Daimler supplied buses to Armstrong-Saurer's home city using Saurer-licence engines.

The railway companies were enthusiastic Dennis buyers, possibly influenced by the fact that Dennis bought shares in some of them! Interestingly, Dennis were Canadian Pacific shareholders too, though whether this helped exports we do not know. The Great Western Railway bought 108 two-tonners like this in 1931, and this example is one of another large fleet owned by the London & North Eastern Railway.

This must have been another sprightly performer – being based on a 65 bhp Dart chassis. Dennis had been making purpose-built

ambulances since 1911, though were unable to wrest the LCC's order for the smaller types away from Talbot. They were soon also to face competition from the cheap and powerful Bedford.

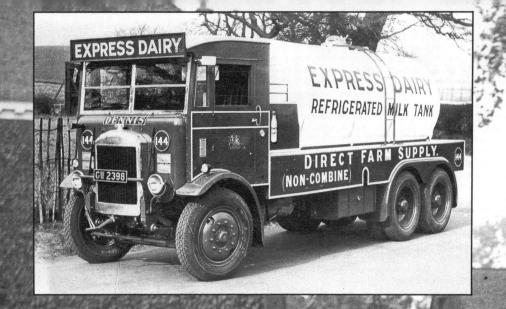

CARLESS, CAPEL & LEONARD · LONDON. E.9.

Pioneers of Petrol

INTERNATIONAL STORES
THE GREATEST GROCERS IN THE WORLD.

CARLESS. CAPEL & LEONARD.

THIS VEHICLE
RUN ON PETROL
Carless Coaline
BRITISH COAL

THIS VEH
S T
Carless Coaline
BRITISH COAL

DENNIS

GH 7547

This and previous three pages: Although the original M Type heavy duty six-wheeler was not a commercial success it was the progenitor of a purpose-built twelve-tonner that did a little better, though it still only accounted for 33 sales before being withdrawn in 1936. Most of these used up the 8 litre side-valve units developed for the abortive M-type bus, but the last two had Gardner diesels and one vehicle was turned out in 1931 with an experimental diesel version of the Arrow engine. Here we see a selection.

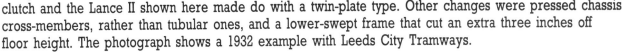

Below: The Lance became known as the Lance I when a simplified Lance II was launched in 1931. Here we have some of the 23 Lance Is purchased by LGOC subsidiary Overground with MCW metal-framed bodies in 1931. Both types, as well as the Arrow, could have four-cylinder 80 bhp engines in place of the normal 100 bhp six-cylinder units.

Left: The Lance I had an almost stall-proof but expensive 14-plate clutch and the Lance II shown here made do with a twin-plate type. Other changes were pressed chassis cross-members, rather than tubular ones, and a lower-swept frame that cut an extra three inches off floor height. The photograph shows a 1932 example with Leeds City Tramways.

Right: A glimpse in the flourishing works at Guildford in 1932 when 32 different models were offered. Many castings and components were brought in from the Midlands by the Southern Railway, though road transport also played its part. Engines were still made at Coventry but even so 10,000 bins of parts were needed for production and spares. Being well away from traditional motor manufacturing areas skilled labour was hard to come by and jigs had to be used for all sorts of relatively simple tasks. Spray painting was utilised for components. Overhead conveyors and trackways on the ground fed parts into the assembly hall.

DENNIS

In 1933 White & Poppe in Coventry was liquidated (its factory being sold to Triumph) and its machinery moved to Guildford. A 21 acre housing estate, Dennisville, was built to accommodate key personnel. This letter shows one of the Dennis family acting as a director in Coventry in the previous year and the problems of engines becoming outdated in the slow sales period of the Depression. P.A. Poppe, who had joined Dennis in 1919, died in 1933 and his sons Gunnar worked for Austin, Olaf for Rover and Erling for Dennis. Jack Milne joined Dennis from White & Poppe, and another recruit at the time was Tom Tillson, who will be referred to again later.

WHITE AND POPPE, LTD.,

MOTOR ENGINEERS,

HOLBROOK LANE,

COVENTRY.

TELEGRAMS
MOTORS, COVENTRY
TELEPHONE,
COVENTRY 8061

ALL COMMUNICATIONS TO
BE ADDRESSED TO THE FIRM
AND NOT INDIVIDUALS

YOUR REF
OUR REF RED/EG.

30th May 1932.

To Messrs. Dennis Bros. Ltd.,
GUILDFORD.

Dear Sirs,

On the 11th March this year we received a Dart engine returned to us together with an official order to be brought up-to-date. This has been done and the engine returned to you.

We have now issued our invoice D.12757 and find that you refuse to pass this item.

Whilst agreeing that this engine is now in a very much better condition than when originally despatched, we cannot agree that no charge should be made for the modifications which we have had to carry out.

Incidentally this engine must have laid in your works for very nearly 2 years.

I shall be glad if you will kindly let me have further particulars so that this invoice may be satisfactorily dealt with.

Yours faithfully,
FOR WHITE & POPPE LTD.,

Director.

P.1238.

This unusual municipal outfit was based on the 2 ton forward-control chassis. The refuse collection trailer for the City of Portsmouth was built by Eagle Engineering of Warwick, which came under the same ownership in 1972 after the Hestair takeover of Dennis.

Municipal business helped to tide Dennis through the Depression of the early 1930s when most of its customers in the haulage field were suffering. Dennis was also popular with 'own-account' transport firms in the South, which tended to fare better than manufacturers in the Midlands and North.

Top: A cheerful-looking driver in breeches (practically jodhpurs!) with his 2 ton Dennis of 1931/2 and a load of milk churns. The moth-eaten state of the photograph is explained by its having been attached with rusty drawing pins to the wall of a transport café on the London to Portsmouth road for some thirty years. A photographer charged drivers for a snap of them with their charges and then gave a copy to the café proprietor. Jack Sparshatt, then a Dennis distributor, managed to rescue this one.

Above: By far the most significant event at Dennis in late 1931 was their famous Lancet passenger chassis. The simple and robust EV had done fairly well and, at a little under £900, was at least £200 cheaper than the sophisticated and slow-selling Arrow. The Lancet was a follow-up to the basic E series theme and was initially offered for only £595. Despite this competitive price, specification was excellent and included Lockheed four-wheel brakes with Marelli servo.

DENNIS

Below: The D3 5.6 litre engine used in the Lancet (which could achieve 11 mpg when laden) was the latest version of the D with various modifications to allow an increase to 2400 rpm, at which 85 bhp was developed. In 1934 Durban ordered a Lancet with a four-cylinder Armstrong-Saurer diesel, and Dennis' own 75 bhp diesel was available in that year with Lanova air-cell combustion head and low-pressure injection It was difficult to start until glow plugs were added. The Arrow six-cylinder engine was also available in a version called the Lancet 6 that cost an additional £100. In 1931 Dennis had examined the Krupp two-stroke diesel and, though this was not adopted, they did offer Dorman-Ricardo and Gardner diesels in some models from 1932, with Perkins available from 1935. It was not until the 0.4 of 1937 that Dennis had much luck with their own diesels.

Opposite page bottom: The Lancet, like its predecessors, was also available with normal control. The first Lancet prototype had been shown at Buenos Aires in March 1931 and it was to the Argentinian market that most bonnetted models were sold. This 1932 example, however, got no further than the Southern Vectis fleet, where it had plenty of more common Dennis types to keep it company. In two years 150 firms and municipalities were running Lancets and a remarkable total of 1,192 had been built when the original model was discontinued in 1937.

Below: Fire appliances had continued to be important business and output had not dropped below 80 per year through the Depression following a record 139 in 1929. This superb limousine type was for Edinburgh in 1932. In 1934 Dennis started to use Meadows engines in their trailer pumps and this make was used from 1939 in some complete vehicles.

P.4062.

WHITBREAD

DENNIS

Whitbread & Co Ltd
Wighthall Brewery,
Quay Street,
Newport, I. of W.

PJ 3753

Left and inset left:
The components of the Lancet were also used in 3^1/$_2$ ton capacity goods vehicles, shown here in 1932 chassis form and in service with Whitbread, whose fleet had now grown to 150 Dennis vehicles of several types. Other large commercial customers at the time included J. Lyons with 90 and United Dairies with 200.

Above:
Quite what this is, apart from being based on a Lancet passenger chassis, is difficult to imagine. It is tempting to say that we are looking at a circus apparatus for firing human cannon balls! The truth is probably more prosaic and the photograph is believed to show a high-powered searchlight. The generator was driven off the engine and was housed behind the cab. What the shed on the back was for is anyone's guess. The London registration places the unusual machine late in 1932.

The forward-control Lancet-based goods chassis was for 4 ton loads and had the D3 petrol engine or else the Dorman-Ricardo 4JUR diesel. Dennis bought one of the latter for evaluation in 1932 and then followed it with 4 in 1933, 16 in 1934, 7 in 1935 and one final engine in 1936. Like the Lancet, this vehicle had hydraulic brakes and very responsive worm and nut steering. It ran nightly from Bermondsey to Burton on Trent.

For lighter public service duties the GL continued in production until October 1933. In all, about 850 G and GL passenger types were produced. This is a 14-seater with Brush bodywork for Coventry in 1932. Some side-valve engines continued to be used into 1932 but most had the ohv 42 bhp engine as used in the two-tonner. The 30 cwt version was the last to receive this shape radiator at the end of 1931.

Erling Poppe, as chief designer, had a difficult brief. Dennis had not done very well in either the heavy truck or double deck bus market in the 1930s and the success of all its lighter vehicles, apart from the Lancet, was being eroded by new mass-produced competitive types like Bedford, Rootes-owned Commer, Dodge and Morris-Commercial. Even Ford had moved into the heavier field. Poppe had to come up with a cheap chassis that offered some of the traditional Dennis advantages of quality. The result was a range of vehicles with pronounced snouts that were soon unofficially known as 'Flying Pigs' or just plain 'Pigs'.

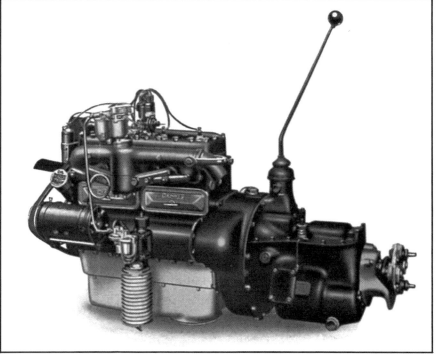

The 'Flying Pig' (officially designated 40/45 cwt for goods and Ace for 20 passengers) cost £260/£285, compared with £245 for the 3 ton Bedford. At its heart was a new rubber-mounted 3.77 litre four-cylinder 60 bhp petrol engine with coil ignition, though a magneto could still be specified for an extra £12. The clutch was initially of cone type running in oil. After years of championing worm drive a spiral bevel axle was used on the grounds that it gave the best combination of ground and floor clearance.

Photographs below: The 40/45 cwt could also be supplied as a trailing-axle six-wheeler for 3¹/₂ ton loads. We see it here in both forward- and normal-control guise. The short wheelbase caused by the set-back front axle made these vehicles surprisingly manoeuvrable and swivel pins with axes at the centre line of the front wheels gave a taxi-type turning circle.

Above: The changing character of household refuse reduced the carrying capacity of traditional dustcarts as weighty ash accounted for a smaller proportion of the payload than bulky packaging, particularly cans. The original Pactum of the early 1930s enabled 13 cu. yds to be crushed sufficiently for 4 to 5 tons to be carried at a time. It was soon followed by this smaller version to suit the 40/50 cwt chassis.

Opposite page top: The Ace-based goods range in 1935 had expanded from just the 40/45 cwt to include a normal-control 35 cwt and forward- and normal-control 50 cwt types. In most cases the differences were largely in price and tyre equipment, wheelbases being either 9ft 6 ins or 11ft 6ins. From 1934 there was also a 70 cwt four-wheeler of similar mechanical specification to take full advantage of the new £30 tax/30 mph class for vehicles of less than $2\frac{1}{2}$ tons unladen weight. Quite which of this bewildering proliferation we have here is difficult to say. However, the horse box body is by Sparshatt, who painted the wood grain effect on the metal cab. As well as the 3.77 litre petrol engine, Dorman-Ricardo and Perkins Leopard diesels were offered.

Below: 4 and 6 ton articulated versions on the Ace theme were also offered. This one is a six-tonner with Hands trailer carrying two 3 ton tanks for powdered fuel. The whole family sold well and some 630 Aces, 5,100 40/45 cwts and nearly 700 70/75 and 80 cwt types had been supplied before the Second World War ended production. There were also almost 1,000 30 cwt vehicles for the Air Ministry delivered early in the War.

Opposite page top: As well as the 20-seat Aces there was the 26-seat Mace (originally to be called Master Ace) of which 84 were made between 1934 and 1937. As can be seen, space for the extra six seats was achieved by using forward-control layout.

Above: With all the interest in light goods vehicles from 1933 the heavyweights seemed to get forgotten. As a result of having no competitive diesel Dennis lost out to the successful Leyland and AEC introductions, as well as to the various firms who had standardised Gardners. Of course, Dennis did fit the latter (for example 11 in 1934 and 51 in 1936) but not surprisingly seemed a little half-hearted in view of the slow gestation of their own types (launched 1931 but not fully sorted out for five years). Here we have a petrol powered six-tonner of 1933.

Left: Between the smallest and largest trucks the Lancet-based types continued. This one had a very low centre of gravity, thanks to the low frame and an elliptical tank, and could have had D3 petrol or Dorman-Ricardo diesel engines. The last four-tonner was made in 1934, this weight class afterwards being catered for by the 3.77 litre types. The smallest of the 'heavy' models then became a five-tonner. In the mid-1930s there was yet more expansion at Guildford, with the erection of No. 11 Shop of 63,000 square feet.

Opposite page top: **Efforts had been made to make the 70 cwt goods model handle a full 4 tons within the £30 tax/30 mph $2^1/2$ ton unladen weight class, but without success. A completely new four-tonner had to be evolved, though the engine and many other components came from its lighter sisters. It first appeared at the end of 1935 and was known as the Light 4 Tonner. 436 had been sold when production ended in 1940. Here we see an early one nearing completion in the Dennis factory. Styling and other features were influenced by the contemporary American Reo and were adopted by the lighter 2-3 ton Ajax introduced in 1937, which however retained the Ace-type radiator shell.**

Left: **Not surprisingly there was a passenger version of the Light 4 Tonner available from 1936. It was known as the Arrow Minor and 45 were sold in its $2^1/2$ seasons. Like the 4 Tonner it could have the new Dennis five-speed gearbox but softer springs and low pressure tyres made it more comfortable than its goods-carrying relation.**

Above: **A way of compressing refuse that also allowed discharge without tipping was the Dennis moving floor. Here a 15 cu. yd capacity machine for Blackpool demonstrates the accessibility of its battery and floor chains. The lines drawn in above the cab seem to indicate that a designer was considering ways of disguising the austere cab roof line. All loading took place in the rear hopper and when full the floor was simply wound forward to leave a new gap for more refuse.**

DENNIS

Right: The Lancet II introduced late in 1935 was designed for the maximum possible number of seats within legal dimensions. 39 passengers could be accommodated, though this Strachan-bodied example had only 32 seats. A new 6.786 litre Big 4 petrol engine, based on Dennis-Lanova components, was used. The latter was redesigned in 1936 as the 0.4 with four valves per cylinder and higher compression. It could achieve 17 mpg with the generally fitted five-speed Maybach gearbox which had a preselective top gear. The automatically servo-activated clutch that had been tried on the Lancet I was available, as was the Gardner 5LW engine. The steering column was almost vertical to gain space and the front was practically flat for the same reason. 780 Lancet IIs were made until the outbreak of the Second World War.

Top far right: Only 53 Lance Is were built but the II did rather better with 219 from its introduction in 1931 to its end ten years later. Its most enthusiastic customers were Walsall with 70, and Aldershot and District with 50 purchased from 1935. This is a 1937 example rebodied in 1947 with East Lancs 48-seat lowbridge body. The Lancet II frontal treatment was also applied to the Lance II in 1935. Engines used in later Lances included the Big 4, 0.4, 5LW, and some in 1940 with the new 0.6 diesel.

Right: A late 1936 'Pig' in unusual form as a road sweeper/sprinkler – others were built as fire appliances. In the following year the three-axle versions of the family were discontinued and the four-wheelers became Ajax 2, 2^1/$_2$ and 3-tonners, looking rather like the Light 4 Tonner shown earlier but with this radiator. Only 102 of the Ajax were built, so the impact of its mass-produced rivals in the lightweight field can be appreciated.

Right:

The Pike psv was based on the mechanical features of the Ajax goods vehicle and was therefore descended from the broadly similar Ace, which also continued in production. It seated 20 passengers and had the usual 3.77 litre petrol engine. Production started in 1938 but ended with the outbreak of war after only 13 had been sold.

Bottom:

An interesting assortment of Dennis vehicles in distributor Sparshatt's workshop in the late 1930s. The Lancet-type bonnetted truck on the left shows how the steering column restricted engine access. An old-type two-tonner and three 'Pigs' are also present. Bodybuilding and painting alongside maintenance must have been unusual even for the 1930s.

Meanwhile, at the Dennis factory the poor sales results of the trucks were largely offset by bus and fire equipment orders, though a serious setback occurred in 1939 with the death of both founding brothers at the ages of only 61 and 68. Sir Raymond had been a suave and persuasive salesman and John a gruff but likeable engineer.

Top far right:

The aptly named Max at the 1937 Commercial Motor Show in London was related to the Lance/Lancet II and had the 0.4 engine. It was designed for the maximum two-axle gross vehicle weight of 12 tons and could carry 7-8 tons depending on bodywork. In 1939 there appeared a 'Chinese six' (a twin-steer 6-wheeler) version for $10^1/2$ ton loads, known as the Max Major. Only two were made, though the type was revived after the War in modernised form.

DENNIS

For 1939 there was a replacement for the Arrow Minor in the shape of the Falcon. It was available with forward control (up to 35 seats) or normal control (20/26 seats). The smaller ones used the 3.77 litre petrol engine, now delivering 75 bhp but others had Gardner 4LK or Perkins P6 units. Only 46 were made pre-War, plus one soon after the War.

A very stylish and modern-looking cab and body built for Northern Aluminium in 1939 by Eagle Engineering. The chassis is a 70 cwt and the coachbuilding is, not surprisingly, in aluminium. It is a pity we do not know the unladen weight, though a payload potential as high as 4 tons seems a reasonable assumption. The futuristic Sunlight van must have been extremely eye-catching when it took to the road in 1934.

Fire appliances of 300-850 gpm became increasingly important at Guildford. Output having averaged 100 per year to 1936, the figure almost doubled in 1937 and there were over 50 trailer pumps ordered by the Home Office as well. Here we see a power operated escape supplied to London in 1937, the year in which the LFB bought their 250th Dennis. From 1937 large (100 x 130 and 110 x 140 mm bore-and-stroke) Meadows six-cylinder engines were used in some, especially in chassis built for Merryweather. 100 such Meadows engines were used up to 1946. Including trailer pumps, output in 1938 was 820 and in 1939 it reached an all-time peak of 2,504. Between 500 and 1,450 fire appliances and trailer pumps were then built in each of the War years up to 1945.

A Five-Tonner (as Dennis not very originally called it) complying with the 30 mph/2$\frac{1}{2}$ ton unladen weight laws was developed in 1939. One version with a very skimpy platform body could very nearly manage 6 tons. During the War 167 were made and the model afterwards became known as the Pax (peace). Here we see a typical normal-control example and also forward-control relatives, all with the latest version of the Ace's petrol engine. PB 5306 is a 1944 vehicle with a cab style that continued after the War. All are delivering petrol for the Pool Board.

DENNIS

Above left: Military versions of several civilian models were built, including 3,000 3 ton tippers and almost 1,000 of these 30/40 cwt trucks for the Air Ministry. Dennis also made the experimental 8 x 8 (also 6 x 6) Octolat with either twin Bedford engines or a single 9.8 litre Leyland. In addition, bombs and bodywork on Dennis and other makes of chassis were produced.

Above right: Vickers no longer had space to make their Carden Loyd light tracked carriers and the work was farmed out to several other companies, including Dennis, during the War. A Ford V8 petrol engine was installed at the rear. Dennis also assembled about 700 Churchill tanks and made tank gearboxes.

Below and opposite page top: Thousands of elderly Dennis vehicles continued to soldier on through the War. Here we see a c1931 two-tonner in its regular state and then fitted with a gas bag on its roof. Several vehicles received this treatment to save using imported fuel and it was appropriate that the Gas Light and Coke Co. should have been early converts to the system.

Below: During the Second World War some 7,000 Dennis trailer pumps worth £400,000 were in use. Since 1934 most of these pumps had used JAP engines in the smaller examples and Meadows 69 x 100 mm bore-and-stroke four-cylinder 'car' engines in the larger types. Here we see three being delivered from Guildford by an old trailing-axle 70 cwt model.

DENNIS

Below: Refuse collectors continued to be of vital importance through the War. This is a 1939 70 cwt type for Croydon showing that streamlining had by now been adopted. Note the typical wartime features of white extremities to aid other road users in the blackout, the headlamp masks and the exhortation to save paper, bones, bottles and scrap iron.

Both photographs opposite page: Two more with the Pool Board, though similar vehicles were also supplied to the Army. These are both examples of the 6/8 ton Max range, of which 1,500 were built during the War. PB 5028 of 1943 has a utility cab, which also sometimes appeared with traditional Dennis radiator style. PB 5153 is a 1944 example with the style of cab used by the Max after the War, albeit by then with a less deep windscreen.

In early 1945 the prototype Lancet III was ready and the Pax goods range soon materialised in forward- and normal-control form. Here we have a 3.77 litre Pax for the Shell Aviation service. The engine was now available either with side valves, developing 70 bhp, or with ohv and developing 10 bhp more. Gross vehicle weight was 19,600 lbs (8,888 kg).

Right:
The normal-control version of the Pax when supplied for articulated work was named the Horla in 1946. This late-1947 example had ingenious bodywork in which the rear half of the roof could be slid over the forward section to facilitate loading.

Opposite page top:
The postwar F series of fire appliances began in 1946 and used Dennis' own petrol engines, with the alternative of Rolls-Royce B80 5.6 litre straight eights developing 150 bhp. The latter could accelerate to 60 mph in 45 seconds and pump 1,000 gallons per minute. This is a 1949 example for Flint. From a 20-year low of only 81 in 1945, fire appliance production grew from 256 in 1949 to 514 in 1951. This was the year when brass finally gave way to chrome.

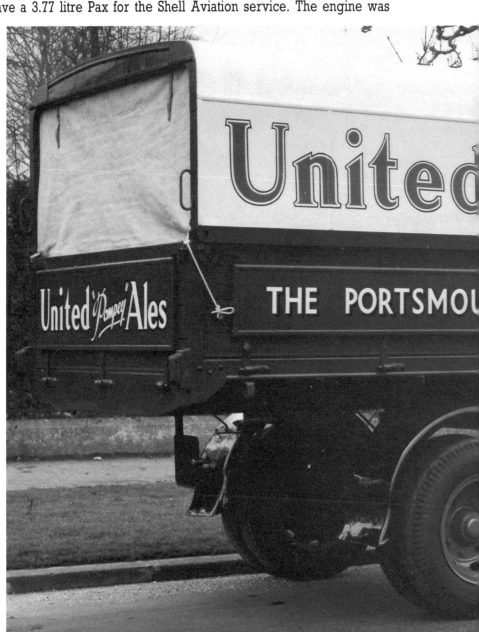

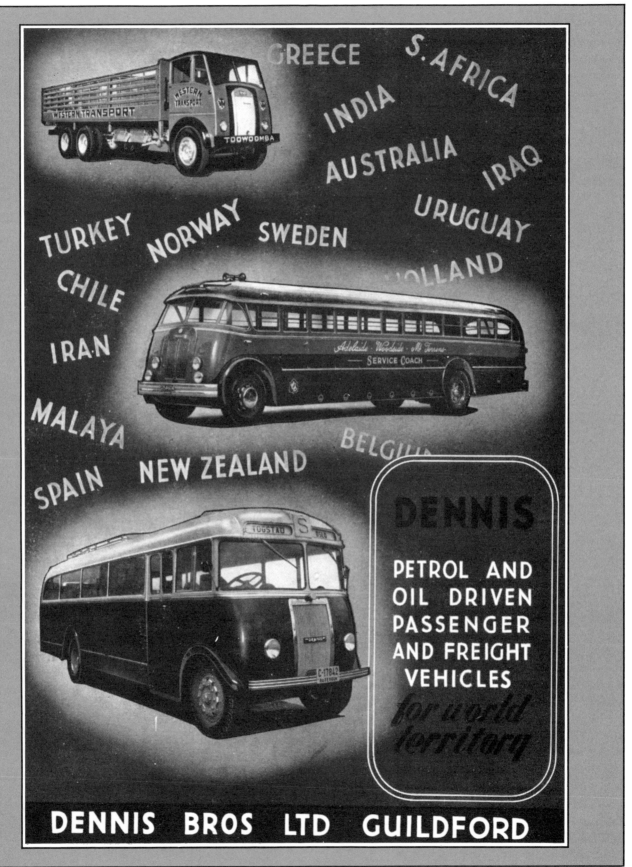

The enormous proliferation of postwar models, and small production of most, means that it will only be possible to examine a representative selection of them. Here we have an advertisement dating from 1951 at a time when motor firms were being forced to export to gain steel quotas. A special export passenger chassis, the Lancet IV, had arrived in 1949 and the Jubilant six-wheeler had been launched at Barcelona three years earlier.

The 0.6 engine developed in 1940 was used in several of Dennis' heaviest postwar models like the Max 6, Jubilant, Lancet III and Lancet IV, Lance, and new underfloor-engined Dominant high-capacity single decker. It had a capacity of 7.58 litres and developed 100 bhp at 1,800 rpm and 315 ft lbs of torque at 1000 rpm. THere were two heads and each cylinder had four valves. A new 5.1 litre six-cylinder diesel was added to the range in 1948, followed by the 5.5 in 1953.

A municipal application of a Pax for Market Bosworth in 1946, but an 800 gallon cesspit emptier requiring a five-man crew plus driver seems unlikely. The explanation is, of course, that in those days many houses had no mains drainage and 'night-soil', as it was coyly described, had to be collected from the cesspit in the garden. Forward-control Pax municipal types included various Paxit variants to replace the old Pactum refuse compression vehicle. Municipal vehicle sales were helped by the arrival of Harold Hattersley, who had been managing director of Karrier.

Erling Poppe had left Dennis and gone on to design, amongst other things, the Sunbeam shaft-driven motorcycle and the Gordon bubblecar. His place as chief engineer had gone to Tom Tillson in 1952, who had joined Dennis 20 years earlier and was later responsible for the rival T-type for Shelvoke & Drewry. Tillson was involved with the Lancet UF (shown here on a 1953 catalogue) which replaced the Dominant and had an underfloor engine, as the initials imply. The rear axle was a newly developed double reduction spiral bevel unit.

The Flat 0.6 diesel used in the Lancet UF was placed in the centre of the chassis and coupled to a five-speed gearbox with pre-selective top ratio. Changes were hydraulically actuated. The engine developed 110 bhp and had the usual four valves per cylinder of its family. Mobile jacks on castors plugged into the engine and, with a few bolts undone, allowed rapid removal.

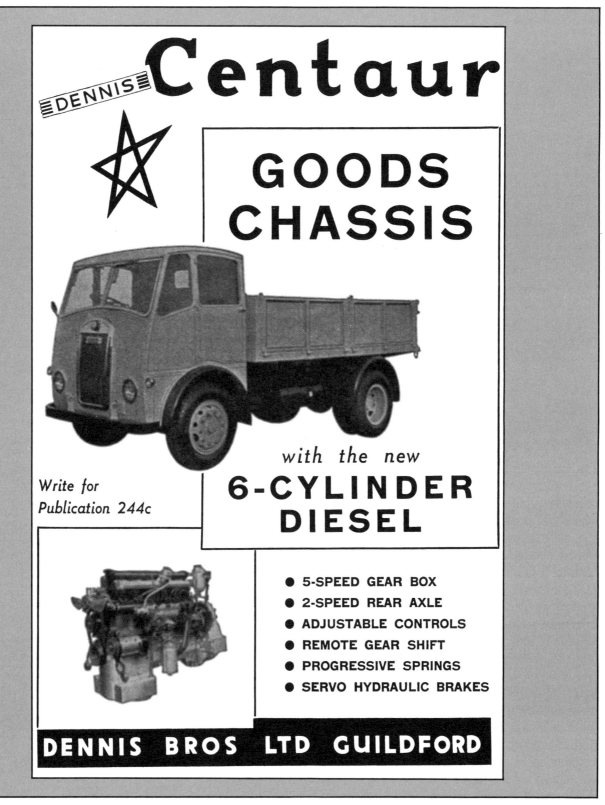

In 1953 the Centaur was the first goods model to receive the new Dennis 5.5 litre 87 bhp six-cylinder engine. This was itself one of the last Dennis diesel types to be designed at Guildford, along with the 8 litre of 1956. The Centaur was intended for 26,888 lbs (12,192 kg) gvw and filled the gap between the Pax and Max.

DENNIS

The traditional wood-framed metal cab built in the Dennis bodyshop received a jolt with the Centaur which was provided with an all-steel design in 1954. However, Dennis hedged their bets and continued to offer the composite type alongside it. The Centaur had a good specification including hydraulic, vacuum servo brakes, two-speed axle and five-speed gearbox.

By the mid-1950s petrol engines were seldom specified and their place was gradually taken in the Dennis range by Perkins units (the accountants running the firm were unwilling to sanction the costly development of new smaller diesels). This is a Teal with P6 engine. It was intended for export (it is shown in Kuala Lumpur,

Malaya) and was more or less a cross between a Pax goods vehicle chassis and a Falcon 30/34-seater.

A remarkably advanced vehicle for 1952 was the Stork, which could be likened to a scaled-down Lancet UF for goods. Its payload was 3 tons and its engine was a horizontal four-cylinder 52 bhp Perkins. Here we have a 1953 example in the unusual role of mobile printing unit for demonstration and practical use at shows and events. Trebor Mints used Storks as mobile showrooms but their use in actual transport was limited. Larger versions with Perkins P6 and Dennis constant mesh gearboxes were soon offered.

New at the 1954 London Commercial Motor Show was Dennis' first design conceived from the outset for ambulance work. The AV1 used a front-mounted Perkins P4 diesel driving a De Dion type rear axle which had Grégoire variable–rate suspension. There was a normal beam axle at the front. The engine was four point rubber-mounted to insulate it from vibrations.

Continuing the bewildering proliferation of new models in the 1950s was the Heron from late 1955. This was a three-tonner in the idiom of the prewar 'Pig' range with a set-forward cab and short wheelbase. The engine was once more a Perkins P4 and was vertically-mounted at the front. It developed 54 bhp and drove through a four-speed synchromesh gearbox to a hypoid bevel axle.

A small number of twin-steer types were built after the War as well as before it. Whether this 1952 example still went under the name Max Major or whether it was regarded as a confused Jubilant is not certain! There was a Max Six but this referred to trucks using the six-cylinder engine.

The popular chairman of Dennis at the time was Sir Geoffrey Burton, who was also a director of Lodge Plugs and Blaw Knox, the construction machinery makers. He died in 1954.

DENNIS

DENNIS *PELICAN*

The Pelican was an underfloor horizontal mid-engined 5.5 litre 92 bhp lightweight bus or coach chassis. It could carry 44 passengers in the former role or 41 plus half a ton of luggage as a coach. Although the engine was manufactured by Dennis much of the rest was not, as it became uneconomic to make so many items for such a wide assortment of models. Amongst the proprietary components was a Meadows gearbox and Moss spiral bevel rear axle.

In 1957 the cab used on the Centaur, Heron, Hefty and others was also offered on the Pax III. A few panels from it were used on this attractive coachbuilt tower wagon built for Blackpool by Eagle Engineering (who were to join with Dennis in the 1970s as part of the Hestair Group).

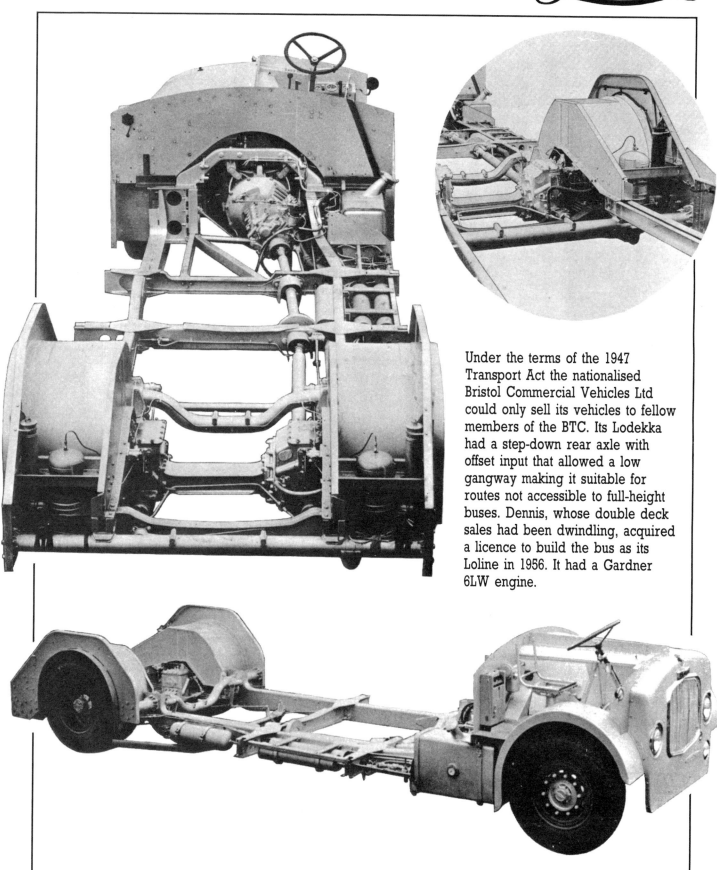

Under the terms of the 1947 Transport Act the nationalised Bristol Commercial Vehicles Ltd could only sell its vehicles to fellow members of the BTC. Its Lodekka had a step-down rear axle with offset input that allowed a low gangway making it suitable for routes not accessible to full-height buses. Dennis, whose double deck sales had been dwindling, acquired a licence to build the bus as its Loline in 1956. It had a Gardner 6LW engine.

Early Lolines had rear entrance bodies, Gardner 6LW engines and Dennis five-speed gearboxes. In 1958 a front entrance version was developed for Walsall Corporation and other engines of 85 to 150 bhp were soon offered, including the 6LX. Four- or five-speed manual or four-speed pneumocyclic gearboxes could be specified. The Loline sold well to a small number of customers, of whom perhaps the most loyal was Aldershot and District with a fleet of 157 in 1964. 50 of these were new Loline IIIs delivered that year.

Opposite page: For truck firms to flourish they need to be surrounded by lots of industry and goods to be transported. When London was an important manufacturing area, rather than just an office district, Dennis had an excellent local market, but by the mid-1950s this had changed. Dennis enjoyed countrywide and export sales of its municipal and fire vehicles but delivery types were increasingly the province of Bedford, Ford, Commer, BMC etc. One area where Dennis continued to enjoy success was with the large number of breweries catering for the London and Home Counties market. Petrol distributors in the area were another group of regular customers.

The cab used on the Heron with roof pressing by Motor Panels of Coventry also spread to the Centaur (1955 example shown here) and the similar Hefty rigid 14 ton gvw four-wheeler that replaced the Max in late 1956. The big Dennis trucks now usually came with Dennis 8 litre diesel or the 8.45 litre Gardner 6LW engines. There was also a similar but smaller Condor with the 5.5 litre Dennis engine.

The Pax was popular with several brewers from 1958 and Dennis made special versions with low decks and 17 inch wheels. Here is an earlier fleet with Watney Combe Reid and Co. at Mortlake. Petrol engines lasted with brewers longer than in most other trades, though Perkins engines were also offered, followed by BMC diesel engines and gearboxes. From 1959 a smoother front wing, bonnet and grille line was achieved by using fibreglass mouldings.

No account of the history of Dennis is complete without a brief mention, at least, of its motor mowers. The first was made in 1922 at roughly the same time that Atco entered the field. Dennis machines mowed the hallowed turf of Lords and Wembley Stadium as well as the lawns of kings and Queen Elizabeth II. In the 1960s it was considered to be so much outside the scope of a vehicle maker that the mower division was hived off, to Godstone Precision Engineering. Here we have a 1960s ride-on example. From 1959 trailed mowers had also been produced.

The Paravan of 1958 was another good idea, but one that appealed to such a small market that it was doomed to commercial failure. The Perkins P4 lived vertically above the front axle, which meant that the driver had clear access to the recessed exit step and to the body behind it. The door rolled upwards, so the vehicle was ideal in congested streets. It was only 6ft 9ins wide and could turn in under 50ft.

Q.5638.

Above and right:

Another contender for the delivery van field, the Vendor of 1960, was even more technically advanced. In common with contemporary continental designs it adopted front wheel drive (just a year after the BMC Mini) and used 2.19 petrol or 2.26 diesel engines by Standard. Payload was 30 cwt and floor height a mere 1ft 7$\frac{1}{2}$ins. There was transverse leaf suspension at the front and rubber at the rear, all being independent. Standard, who had recently entered the heavier van field, was impressed and considered buying Dennis, though principally for its name and sales network.

A 1962 Paxit followed by a long-lived 1944 predecessor with Fulham Borough Council. The Pax-based municipal vehicles had included maximum weight types since the Paxit Major of 1952 and diminutive 7/8 cu. yd refuse collectors. The smallest 7ft 6in. wheelbase chassis with P4 or Dennis 3.77 litre petrol engine was also used for tower wagons, trucks and 600 gallon gulley emptiers from the mid-1950s.

By 1960, when Brian Stacey succeeded Tom Tillson as chief engineer, the Pax range was available with over eighty variations of wheelbase, engine, transmission etc. In an effort to simplify this and reduce production costs a Pax IV was developed alongside restricted Pax II and III ranges. The new fibreglass cab shown here dated from late 1960 and was soon applied to the whole range. Here we have a Perkins 6.305 engined 5 ton tipper for the County Borough of Walsall. Other Pax models had BMC and AEC/Maudslay engines.

DENNIS

A pause for breath with a varied assortment of ages and shapes of fire appliance spanning over 20 years with Surrey Fire Brigade.

The situation at Dennis in the 1960s was becoming critical. The fire appliances and municipal types sold well, but not well enough to support a large general truck and bus factory. The fire equipment section of Alfred Miles Ltd was bought in 1962, followed in 1964 by the Mercury tug firm, purchased for £140,000. However, financial losses in the mid 1960s put the company in a vulnerable position. We have already seen that Standard considered buying Dennis, and other interested parties were Tecalemit and Thornycroft. The latter had 2,000 small diesel engines to dispose of, but were themselves acquired by AEC in 1961.

DENNIS

Right and below: An interesting idea following the takeover of Alfred Miles (whose parent company had made aircraft refuellers) was a low-level tanker based on the Delta fire chassis, also shown with ultra-low cab that allowed a snorkel arm to ride above it.

The Tecalemit takeover previously mentioned failed to materialise when in 1969 a revaluation showed that the Dennis works was worth £1.5 million more than its book value. One outcome was that I.G.H. Wilson of Tecalemit got to know the Dennis board, where there had been several changes as the economic plight worsened, and he became managing director in 1969.

Opposite page bottom: after the production of Mercury trucks was moved from Gloucester to the Dennis factory in 1964/5, there was even a joint family resemblance. This is a MDT 3 three-tonner for 6,000 lb (2,721 kg) loads and was available with either Ford 122E petrol or Perkins 4.99 38 bhp diesel engines. Some pre-Dennis versions of this vehicle had actually been sold as Mertruck refuse collectors.

Above: In 1964 Dennis launched its Maxim range of two-axle trucks to take full advantage of the new 16 ton rigid and 32 ton articulated vehicle weight limits. There was also a 20/22 ton six-wheeler. Production started in 1965 and the engine used was the Cummins VALE 185 bhp V-8 with Dennis five-speed gearbox and optional two-speed axle. The engine was noisy and not very satisfactory in this application and, although the truck was cheap, it did not sell well. The chassis shown here carried 11 tons and was listed at £3,290 plus body and £320 for the double-skin fibreglass cab.

Opposite page top: At first sight this 1966 van looks like a Heron or Stork but is in fact a Paravan without its recessed nearside corner. Sales of the lighter Dennis models apart from the Pax had virtually ceased and the Maxim had not done at all well. This was largely because of operator suspicion of the new V8 diesel and, because sales of the Hefty and Jubilant models had been low for many years, Dennis had little hope of fleet replacement orders against the entrenched heavy vehicle specialists.

Opposite page bottom: The light bus field still interested Dennis and it continued to try various models. This is a 1965 Pax IIA with 5 litre Perkins 89 bhp diesel and Dennis five-speed gearbox. The body was built by Dennis itself and seated 32 passengers.

The Pax V low-loading six-wheeler was launched at the Scottish Motor Show in late 1963 with brewers
very much in mind. It came as a trailing-axle six-wheeler or a twin-steer type. The engines offered were
the Perkins 6.354, AEC 7.7 or Gardner 5LW. About 125 four-cylinder AEC 5.1 litre engines developed
by Maudslay were also used in some four-wheel brewery vehicles. The illustrations show a 1965 Flowers
vehicle and dimensions chart for the twin-steer type.

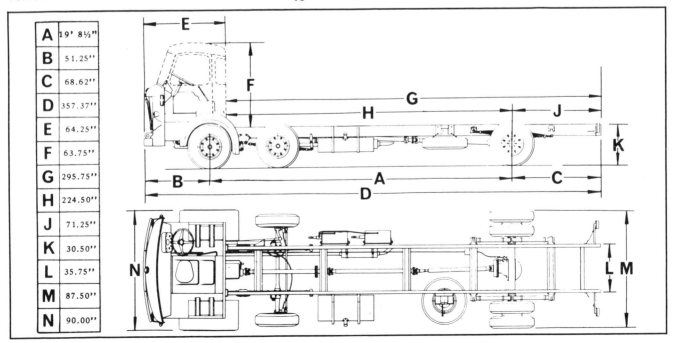

A	19' 8½''
B	51.25''
C	68.62''
D	357.37''
E	64.25''
F	63.75''
G	295.75''
H	224.50''
J	71.25''
K	30.50''
L	35.75''
M	87.50''
N	90.00''

An ingenious mid-1960s idea was the Dennis Extricator. It was cheaper and simpler than a lockable differential and less likely to be abused and cause damage to the transmission. It consisted of an axle with grooved wheels that could be screwed against the tyres, thus overcoming differential action if the twin wheels on one side were spinning. It was intended particularly for fire appliances and municipal vehicles that only occasionally had to leave metalled roads. Dennis were also willing to build bodies on other people's chassis at the time, hence the Karrier-Dennis.

A 1967 Pax V with the new bolder lettering adopted by Dennis. This machine for Bury had Edbro lifting equipment to tackle a new menace for local authorities–abandoned cars.

DENNIS

In 1967 Dennis decided to capitalise on the Maxim's principal asset, its light weight. They replaced the troublesome VALE engine with a 170 bhp Perkins V8, which only gave sufficient power for 30 ton operation. This, however, was no great problem as the Maxim's low unladen weight actually meant that it could carry more payload at 30 tons gvw than the typical 32-tonner. Before the re-launch it had been offered at 28 tons, when this advantage was less evident.

To test its claims, John Moon of *The Commercial Motor* took a Perkins-powered Maxim over the Alps to Italy in 1967 and was favourably impressed. He admitted to feeling rather a long way from the nearest Dennis and Perkins backup facilities, but fortunately neither was needed. The Maxim's two-speed double reduction Centrax axle gave it ten ratios to tackle the steepest hills and a 54 mph top speed on the level.

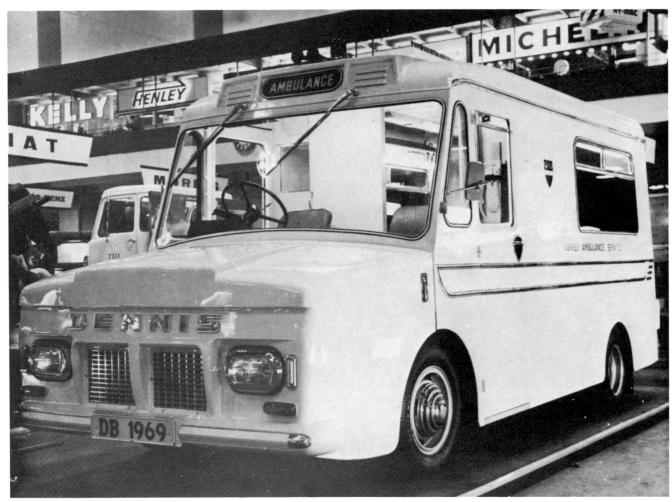

At the 1968 Commercial Motor Show Dennis came up with a highly sophisticated ambulance incorporating many of the lessons

learned from the Vendor's front wheel drive. However, this was a much more powerful vehicle with a Jaguar 2.8 litre six-cylinder engine and automatic transmission. It was understandably expensive and few local authorities could afford to buy examples.

By the late 1960s open-cabbed fire appliances were a thing of the past in Britain but still specified for some overseas customers like Johannesburg, South Africa. This is an F44 with Rolls-Royce petrol engine shown on test in England before despatch.

Mercury Model MD30, operating as part of an integrated materials handling system, tows a load of industrial power units.

THE RANGE OF MERCURY TRUCKS AND TRACTORS

MD 20 & MD 30
D.B.P. 2,000 &
3,000 lb.
907 & 1,361 kg.

MD 40 & MD 60
D.B.P. 4,000 &
6,000 lb.
1,814 & 2,721 kg.

MD 100 & MD 130
D.B.P. 10,000 &
13,000 lb.
4,536 & 5,897
kg.

AIRTUG MD 300
D.B.P. up to 30,000 lb.
13,608 kg.

SHUNTUG 70
Moves up to
200 tons on
level rails.
203,208 kg.

T3 TRUCK
Carries up to
6,000 lb.
2,721 kg.

MERCURY TRUCK & TRACTOR CO. LTD
Woodbridge Works, Guildford, England. Telephone: Guildford 5291

Member of the **DENNIS** *Group*

Printed in England 1½m 7/67

Brunnings

A 1967 leaflet for the Mercury range, showing one at work in the Dennis factory and part of the range. As can be seen, some Dennis fibreglass mouldings were being used. Following the Hestair takeover, Mercury was sold in 1972 and joined forces with another tug and industrial maker to form Reliance-Mercury, based in Halifax.

Above and right:
The final version of the Pax V for goods was revised in 1971 as the DB15.5, which to confuse matters, was sometimes called the Dominant (as were some earlier bus models). A Dominant cesspool emptier is also shown. Both had a six-cylinder 120 bhp Perkins diesel and the haulage model was for 15$\frac{1}{2}$ tons gwv, at which it could carry more than the average 16 tonner, yet pay less road tax.

An articulated version of the 15.5 was developed with turbocharged version of the same engine developing 155 bhp. It drove through a five-speed gearbox to a two-speed axle. Styling was slightly revised and a new model name chosen, the Defiant DB24T. At only 4 tons 4 cwt kerb weight for the tractor, the outfit could carry half a ton more than most rivals at 24 tons gtw.

The Pax V carried on into the 1970s for municipal work. This 13 ton gvw example is for street washing and gulley emptying. We have already noted that several suitors considered buying the Dennis firm, one of the last being Seddon in 1969 before they settled for Atkinson instead in 1970. As it was, a saviour came in 1972 in the shape of Hestair, who paid £3.4 million. Other members of the group included municipal equipment makers Eagle Engineering and Yorkshire Vehicles (the former steam wagon maker).

A low-level Snorkel chassis sets out to Cleveland from Woodbridge Works (the 'Hill' in its name having been discontinued in the 1930s). The signs behind it show one of the ways that Hestair raised money to revive the Dennis operation. They sold off much of the factory and then leased back just the part that was actually needed for a smaller output of 15 vehicles a week from a workforce of 300. By the mid 1970s production had doubled and parts of the factory were reoccupied and in 1978 the 32 acres factory was re-purchased.

A 1973 Alleycat compression refuse collector. As its name implies, this was a very compact machine in the tradition of the old 40/45 cwt and smallest Pax, for congested back streets. With a new Ogle styled steel cab it was revised for the 1980s as the smallest of a range of Phoenix refuse collectors with a width of only 2 metres. A similar compact chassis but with turbocharged Perkins T6 was also used for the DS fire appliance.

Left:
Fire appliance production reached 400 per year in the mid 1970s. This is a 1976 F series model available with either Rolls-Royce 235 bhp 6.5 litre straight eight petrol engine or Perkins 185 bhp V8 diesel. Smaller D models had Perkins 155 bhp T6 diesel or Jaguar 4.2 litre petrol engines.

Opposite page bottom: In 1977 Dennis staged a successful comeback as a bus manufacturer with the Dominator double decker. This had a transverse, rear-mounted Gardner 6LW with Voith three-speed automatic gearbox, which had a built-in retarder (with the option later of the ingenious Maxwell-Brockhouse four-speed transmission). A front-engined Jubilant, primarily for export, was also developed. Sales were handled by Bob Crouch, formerly of Daimler.

Above: The Firebird was a simple water tender primarily for export that could be fitted to Dennis or other chassis. It could have tanks of 600 to 1,000 gallons capacity and a 600 gpm pump. When fitted to the Delta chassis, as shown here in 1977, it could be powered by Perkins V8 or six-cylinder diesel, or various petrol engines. At the time Dennis also built fire/crash tender bodywork on Thornycroft 6 x 6 chassis and 'first strike' appliances on the Land-Rover.

Top: Another export special of the late 1970s. In several markets the traditional fibreglass Dennis cab was unacceptable and this steel type manufactured by Motor Panels of Coventry was substituted, incorporating Dennis' own frontal styling. Having concentrated on exports (worth almost £13 million in 1977) and municipal vehicles for the British market, Dennis returned to the goods vehicle field in 1978 with the Delta 16-tonner. A further development at this time was the production of Dennis designs in Cyprus, under the designation KMC.

Dennis' success in the modern bus market has been achieved by exploiting gaps left by bigger manufacturers and building special designs to customer order. Over 1,000 of its new generation buses had been sold by 1983. Recent models have included the Falcon single decker (shown in Leicester livery) and its double deck counterpart, launched in 1981 with rear-mounted Gardner or Mercedes-Benz V6 diesel; the Dart single decker with front-mounted Perkins V8, new in 1978; the Dominator, shown previously; the front-engined Jubilant double decker; and the Lancet shown here. The latter is a straight-framed vehicle with mid-mounted Perkins, Leyland, Gardner or Rolls-Royce 124-230 bhp diesels, and is available with automatic or manual transmission, leaf or air suspension, and in several chassis lengths and wheelbases.

The 1980s also saw a return by Dennis to the coach market, and both mid- and rear-engined types were produced. This is the Dorchester chassis with horizontal mid-mounted Gardner 230 bhp diesel (other outputs and also Rolls-Royce types available), and ZF six-speed gearbox (SCG or Voith optional). It could have leaf or air suspension and was designed for use with 10, 11 or 12 metre bodywork. The 12 metre example shown has a Berkhoff body and is seen at Windsor.

Above: The new Ogle-designed modular steel tilt-cab with aluminium and fibreglass lower panels was built in various configurations for municipal chassis, as well as for a new version of the Delta 16-tonner (previously provided with fibreglass cab) announced in 1978. Initially, powered by a Perkins T6 155 bhp diesel, it was joined in 1981 by a Gardner 6LXB 180 bhp version, of which 20 are in service with Hinchliffe. Both types have six-speed overdrive synchromesh gearboxes. A three-axle Phoenix refuse collector, destined for the Middle East, is also shown with a similar cab.

Left: About 40 six-wheeled Condor and Dragon buses had been constructed for Hong Kong by early 1984. They could accommodate about 170 passengers and have a Gardner/Voith combination similar to the Dominator. Some found service with the Kowloon Motor Bus Company and others with the China Motor Bus Co. This example has a body by Duple Metsec (now in the Hestair empire).

Above: Refuse collection chassis and bodywork formerly built at Guildford were concentrated at Hestair Eagle in Warwick in 1986. Warwick was also the base for Yorkshire cesspit and gully emptiers formerly produced in Leeds and available on a variety of chassis makes. Shown is the latest Phoenix 8-II able to carry eight tons of compressed garbage on an extremely compact chassis. Hestair has over fifty per cent of the municipal vehicle market in Britain and, in addition to its own bodywork, some two or three Dennis chassis go to other makers of refuse collection bodywork each week. Hestair Eagle's own bodywork is built almost exclusively from 50B abrasion-resistant steel and there is a growing use of three axle chassis with maintenance-free rubber suspension.

Opposite page: The virtual collapse of the bus market in Britain in the 1980s led to major rationalisation in the Hestair Group, where Dennis was making only one chassis per week in 1986. The Duple bodyworks in Blackpool also belonged to Hestair and was making a small number of complete integral vehicles in addition to coachbuilding on chassis from other sources. To make better use of its surplus capacity, Duple became cab manufacturer for Dennis in 1986, as well as producing Metsec body kits for assembly overseas–a notable customer being Hong Kong, which had bought over eight hundred Dennis vehicles in the previous eight years. Shown here is a Belgian Van Hool bodied Lancet Alizee highline midi coach with 150 bhp Perkins diesel and ZF six speed gearbox.

Having moved the bulk of production to Warwick and Blackpool, Hestair drastically reduced the size of the Guildford operation where annual theoretical output was 1500 vehicles per year, but land had become worth a million pounds an acre to developers. 450 jobs were lost (though 250 were added at other sites) and 300 remained at Guildford in a modernised factory making PSV and fire appliance chassis. These were then despatched elsewhere for completion, the majority of the fire chassis going to Carmichaels of Worcester. The machine depicted is the latest addition to the range of RS full width water tenders, DS narrow track water tenders, Delta I special purpose chassis and DF sixteen ton specialist models. It is the SS with tilting steelcab, various Perkins engine options and manual of automatic transmission. Dennis is now in a leaner, stronger position to face the 1990s and its centenary.